Sacred Eye
Poetry in Search of the Divine

Heather —
Love & Peace —
Rev. Bill M—
March 25, 2023

The book cover's design by Allen Gandy was selected by The American Authors' Association as a Gold Book Award winner for book cover design.

Edited by Jan Hornung—author, editor, helicopter pilot
http://www.geocities.com/vietnamfront

© Copyright 2004, W.H. McDonald Jr.
All rights reserved.

No part of this book may be reproduced, stored in a retrieval system, or transmitted by any means, electronic, mechanical, photocopying, recording, or otherwise, without written permission from the author.
ISBN: 1-59457-239-9

To order additional copies, please contact us.
BookSurge, LLC
www.booksurge.com
1-866-308-6235
orders@booksurge.com

Sacred Eye

Poetry in Search of the Divine

W. H. McDonald Jr.

2004

Sacred Eye
Poetry in Search of the Divine

Dedicated To:

- My friends from the **Self-Realization Fellowship** in Sacramento

- All the friends I have met at **Angel Fire,** New Mexico

- The men and brothers living at **The Hidden Valley Ashram**

- To my **Vietnam Veteran brothers**, both living and dead

Table of Contents

Acknowledgements	xv
Foreword	xvii
Introduction	xix
POEMS	xxi
The Sacred Road	1
The Raven Speaks …Yet Only the Mountain Knows	2
Messengers	4
Angels Have Faces Too	5
Love is Like Peanut Butter	6
Holographic Gurus	7
A Footprint in the Dust	8
The Prophets Said Life was Beautiful	9
Ascension	10
The Mute Night	12
On the Edge of the Fire	13
Fall	14
Footprints and Reincarnation	15
Sitting at a Paris Café—1965	16
Lover by the Sea	18
I Learned to Love the Rain	19
Raven Dances	21
Men are Not Mountains	23
Church Steps	24
Conversations with Mirrors	25
Journey Back to Light	27
Costumes	29
Beaches	30
UFOs in Central Park?	31
Vacation Memories	33
No Golden Roof	34
Thoughts While Hitchhiking	36
I Sit in the Darkness	37
Rosary Beads	38

Photograph Image Within	39
Mary	41
Monks Do Not Fear Darkness	42
Wildflower	43
Solitary Journeys	44
The Rain Falls	45
Angels R Us	46
Gypsies and Butterflies	47
Indian Cliff Dwellings	48
The Piano Man	50
Winter Chill	51
Quasimodo	52
Do You Really Hear Me?	53
Reunion	54
Not Enough	55
Security Blanket	56
Sabotage	57
Submarines	58
The Image in the Mirror	59
Handyman	60
Minefield of Emotions	61
The Wind	62
Surface Roots	63
Risk Taking	64
Which Way?	65
The Dancers	66
Children Dance	67
It Has Been a Long Time	68
City Streets	70
Summer Mornings	71
Working in the City	72
I Read Somewhere Once	73
Peeling Onions	74
They Say	75
Unrequited Love	76
Found	77
Before	78

The Ice Queen	79
Restless	80
Airport 2001	82
Breakfast Conversations	83
Earth Angel	84
Auto Mechanic	85
Abandoned	86
The Desert	87
Be Real	88
Inner Skies	89
School of Light	90
Distance Between the Births	91
Journey of Doubts	92
Desires	93
Circular Lights	94
I Found Different Shores	95
Poets Have Faith and Believe in Everything	97
You Were My First Love	99
I Wonder Where Elvis is Tonight?	100
My Friend Went Back to the Stars	102
The Sea Gives Back	104
Words are Only Vehicles Between Moments in the Silence	105
The Sky Follows Us-It Never Asks Why	106
The Pathways Are Not Always Marked With Signposts	107
The Owl Angels	109
Angels, A-bombs, and the Wind	110
The Past is Dead	111
Emotions are Just Tracks of Tears	112
A Dream Without Any Sunshine	113
Clouds Do Not Own the Sky	114
Points in Time	115
Time Will Tell	116
He Might Have Been a Saint	118
Tibetan Words Chanted Within, in an Overture to God	120
Awakening!	122
Inca Medicine Wheel	123
No One Can Really Know Paris	125

Saw a Young Child	126
Fabric of Life	127
Inner Poetry is Not for the Critics	129
About the Author	131

Other books by W. H. McDonald Jr.:
A Spiritual Warrior's Journey—The Inspiring Life Story of a Mystical Warrior
Purple Hearts—Poetry of the Vietnam War

Contributing author to the following books:
Angels in Vietnam: Women Who Served by Jan Hornung
Spinning Tails: Helicopter Stories by Jan Hornung

Documentary film appearances and participation in:
In the Shadow of the Blade

Acknowledgements

Thank you to **Allen Schmeltz** who has always encouraged and enjoyed my poetry; your supportive words over the years have helped create this volume of spiritually-based poems.

Thanks to **Jan Hornung** who continues to be my literary shadow when it comes to writing and creative thought. Her ongoing support is more than even she realizes. Her energy is instilled throughout this book.

Thanks to **Patty Biegun Hancock** are not enough for the spiritual friendship that has inspired me these past couple of years.

For all his work on my book cover, thank you to **Allen Gandy**. I appreciate the many hours of work and exchange of ideas to create what was the perfect award-winning design. Thanks!

For inspiration from old friends: **Anne Franklin, Sarah Judi Grant, Bob Amick, Karen Wilson, Mahaila McKellar,** and **Dondee Nettles**.

Carol; for your loving support all these years—thank you!

My life and my poetry would be incomplete if it were not shared with my grandchildren, **Jesse, Spencer,** and **Daylana**.

Foreword

> I wish I were
> A huge rain cloud;
> I'd burst upon the earth
> And cleanse mankind.
>
> Alas, I am a single
> Raindrop
> That must join forces
> To make the summer rains.
> by Jan Hornung

Bill McDonald weaves a satin ribbon-message of love as "the eternal light that never fades" throughout his book of life's poetry. With homeless souls, gurus, and mystical sages as his muses, he orchestrates the rhythm of the sea's tides and the grace of "waltzing ravens" into his poetic art form. He metaphorically turns "moths flirting with cremation" and butterflies "in search of rainbows" into rhetorical comments on all of our lives as he reminds us that "all of life is in rhythm with the rain."

Bill choreographs the flight of owls, ravens, and angels in his verse as he poses existential reflections on religion, relationships, and rebirth. Combining despair and hope in one breath, he tugs at our heartstrings by telling us that "we will never feel what the rose feels." He challenges our thinking by asking, are angels "all around us or do they dwell within?" And he tickles our funny bones as he wonders, "Do (angels) fly or take the bus?" Let Bill take you through his "minefield of emotions" as he effectively and persuasively weaves you into "the fabric of (his) heart."

Discover love, truth, hope, peace, and God through Bill's poetry as he shows you that "poets have faith and believe in everything." Find your own *Sacred Eye* as you *Search for the Divine* through the poetry of Bill McDonald.

Jan Hornung
Author/editor, Huey pilot, Army wife
Angels in Vietnam: Women Who Served
This Is The Truth As Far As I Know, I Could Be Wrong
If A Frog Had Wings...Helicopter Tales
KISS the Sky...Helicopter Tales
Spinning Tails: Helicopter Stories

Jan Hornung is at http://www.geocities.com/vietnamfront

Introduction

Some of these poems have been written and kept in dark, dusty places for decades while others were shared with selected friends. Each of these poems represents a piece of my own soul as I grew and changed and saw the world around me. It was all a part of the spiritual evolutionary process called life. To grow and to change is to stay alive and free of stagnation and mental and emotional death.

Poetry is an outer coat of words that a poet chooses to wear in public or in private. It is a reflection of the inner self. It is a look at the world of delusion through the poet's "sacred eye." Seeking understanding with the surrounding environment and people, the poet uses poetry to find his own enlightenment. The poet becomes one with what he writes and merges his emotional and spiritual self into words that can be read.

These poems may not mean what you think even when it seems clear that the simple thoughts and words are just what the poet was expressing. Do not go so quickly into an understanding—look within yourself for deeper meanings. Real poetry speaks to your heart and to your higher self. Listen to yourself. Hear what the words cannot convey fully. For some feelings there are never enough words to fully express what the poet means, while some thoughts and observations can be expressed in just one word—love!

Read and enjoy, and come back later and read them again; you will find new meanings that you did not have when you first read them.

God bless each of you that should read my humble words. Poetry is the food for the soul. Let your spirit eat and enjoy!

W. H. McDonald Jr.

POEMS

Poetry is the very soul of life. It is the sacred eye of the heart.
It is food for the creative process. It is love. It is God's voice!
W. H. McDonald Jr.

The Sacred Road

The heart sometimes
Leaves an easy trail to follow,
Like footprints in the newly fallen snow.
I know where I have been,
All I have to do is look at the tracks
Made by my heart.

I know so little about us.
No matter how close we sleep together,
Or how much we talk,
I never really know what is inside
Just behind your dark brown eyes.
I never know where I stand
In your dreams
And in your desires.
I never know how deeply
You drink from my heart's well.

In time, I will not question us,
Nor worry about the sunrises
That will bring more light to our life.
I have you now.
At this very moment,
That is all I need.
That is all I ever needed!

The Raven Speaks ...
Yet Only the Mountain Knows
A Grand Canyon Experience April 1997

The very breath
Of spiritual life
Flows through these vast canyons
Resting between walled-mountain arms.
Down below
In the dark shadows
Ravens soar
As they listen
To the voices
Of long ago.

The sky touches
The top of the horizon,
Holding onto it
Like a mother
Holding her small child.

The sun dances gently above,
Making the snow-covered canyons
Sparkle like jewels
Hung on a rock wall.

I search the vastness
And seek to know it
As well as the raven,
But I am limited
To view this moment
Only as a visitor.

This morning lives
Only to please.

There is no place
For a closed heart
Or troubled thoughts.
My spirit
Soars with the raven.

We are bonded together
In this moment,
One with the spirit lands.
One with the past.
I can feel
Ancient brothers within.
I know them in this place
As I walk
Where they once journeyed.

I look skyward
And feel the spirits in the sky.
I gaze out across the valleys
And know
That their God
And mine
Are one in the same.

Brother raven,
Bird of many visions
And dreams,
Like a ghost-dancer across time,
I open my heart to you.
Hear my silent prayers
For my Mother Earth
And Sister Sky.

Messengers

Messengers
Are like pockets;
Neither is comfortable
With its own self
Unless filled
With a message
Or a warm hand.

I came to see you.
But you took
The moment away
Without as much as a thought,
And the message
Became lost and unwelcome.

I stood there feeling
Like empty pockets
And old lint,
Wanting to cry.

Angels Have Faces Too

When I saw my wife
Look at our son,
I knew love's deepest secret:
That to know real love
You must become a mother
With large brown angel-eyes
And an angel face.

I saw the joy
In her love
And knew
That no husband
Or father
Could ever
Share
Or know
Such a moment.

If angels have faces,
Then sometimes they must
Look just like mothers.
Sometimes they might
Even look like wives.
But sometimes,
There is no difference.

I know,
I saw
An angel
And she
Was my wife
And mother
Of our son!

Love is Like Peanut Butter

I used to love you
Almost as much
As crunchy
Peanut butter.

I was so much
Younger then.

I did not realize
How good
You could taste
Spread out
On a sandwich
Of beach sand and sky.

Now,
I must admit
That my tastes have changed,
However, I still like you better
Than peanut butter
Most of the time,
But it is close.

Holographic Gurus

I stepped outside
Of myself yesterday
And found *now*
Waiting for me.
I saw within
The golden haze
A dark-skinned yogi
Smiling at me.

He greeted me
Without saying a word.

Then I understood
That all visions
And all gurus
Are within us already,

If we just
Step outside our thoughts
To see
And to listen.

A Footprint in the Dust

Sometimes
Someone says something
That lays a footprint
On the surface of my memory,
Much like those
That were fossilized on the moon
By lonesome
Astronauts.

When I awoke
This morning
And saw you standing
Silhouetted against the dawn's
Morning light,
I heard you whisper my name.

It sounded like
The music one hears
Only within seashells
Or dreams.
It sounded
Like love.
It sounded
Like us.

The Prophets Said
Life was Beautiful

Love lies hidden
In the quietness
Of the rocks
And on beaches
Where no one has yet to walk
Or has even touched
With their dreams.

Love is hidden on cloudy days
And in darkened skies,
Needing only to be discovered
By young lovers
Huddled up
In the warmth
Of each other.

They do not need windows to see
That love is a cousin of the wind.
It can be felt
But not easily seen.

Ascension
The Grand Canyon 1997

Returning rivers
To the womb of the sea,
Stopping only long enough
To take a part of us
From the canyon walls
Of our heart.

I look down from the edges
Of your journey
And see the traces
Of your wanderings
Through time.

I wonder
How many others have stood here
Before me
Seeking answers within?

I hear the drums
Of the Hopi
And the singing of the ravens.
I hear the songs of the gods within.

I cry out to the raven,
"Must we all return
Like the Colorado River,
Carving paths
And creating canyons
In the hearts and minds of others
On our countless journeys
To and from the womb?"

Then the raven whispered back to me,
"None of this is real.
We have never
Left the womb.
All is delusion.
You are free to soar
And to ascend to the heavens.
No one is forever
Trapped in the canyon lands
Of the soul."

The Mute Night

The moon encircled
By a misty glow
And us
Enclosed in loving arms
With thoughts of
Wonders and miracles
That this night
May bring.

Oh, somewhere
Poets are writing
Unhappy verse
And drowning
On their depressed prose
Of lost love.

But you and I
Share this moment
Under a night sky
Filled with starry-eyed witnesses
While the earthen womb
Under our feet
Confesses to love both of us.

What more could we
Ever ask
Of any night?

On the Edge of the Fire

I've danced with fire
On my own highway of desire.
I've stood by
Watching how others
Got drawn into
Those hot flames
Like moths
Flirting with cremation.

Oh yes, I was tempted
To reach out and embrace
Those roaring fires too!
But so far,
I've managed to step back
From the edge
And avoid seriously burning
My apprentice angel wings.

However, I must admit
To being close enough, on occasion,
To get some
Smoke in my eyes!

Fall

How did God,
Just sit there,
Watching all those angels
That fell to earth,
Without shedding
So much as a tear?

I cried last night
Looking outside
From my window
As fallen raindrops
And leaves
Just laid there,
Dying
All alone
On that cold, wet sidewalk.

Footprints and Reincarnation

Didn't we just walk on this beach
Yesterday?
Where are all our footprints
That carried us across
This sandy shore?

There are
No traces
Left to mark
Our place
In time or space.
The tides have
Washed all the evidence away
Of any previous journeys.

Sometimes
I wonder if
I lived before
On other beaches
In some other time?

Just because the tides
Have washed away
All the footprints
Doesn't mean
I wasn't there.

Sitting at a Paris Café—1965

I stare across my table
And warm coffee
At the mass of people drifting
Across my view.

They go by me
As if life
Had more meaning than
Just a journey of the heart.

I see some dressed in business suits
And expressions of fear—
Fear of tomorrow,
Of today,
Of the tax man,
And death.

Lovers strolling past, hand in hand,
Going somewhere,
But it seems to not matter where.

Hordes of faceless people searching
For that road sign that points the way
To any exit from here.

I sip my coffee and scan the view
For friendship and love
That might pass me by.

It is a tired and endless highway
Of eyes, all afraid to look into mine,
All afraid of what others think and say.
They keep moving,

Never stopping to
Connect with me
At my little table
On a sidewalk
In Paris.

Lover by the Sea
Hawaiian Islands, July 1964

Lover by the sea,
You came to me
And wrote poems
And wove dreams
Upon my sandy mind.

The footprints
Of your passion
Still dances within,
Beyond the reach
Of the hungry tide.

I Learned to Love the Rain

I love the music of the morning
As raindrops
Beat out their rhythms
On my bedroom windowpanes.

I have heard that beat before
Under tin roofs
In faraway jungles
Where lonesome young warriors,
Not understanding
The rhythms of the rain,
Nor life,
Cried to the beat
Of that falling rain.

Now I am lying here
Next to you.
I have no fears.
No anger.
No worries
About bombs
Or tomorrows.

I have learned to love
The rhythm of the rain.
I have learned to love you.
I have learned to love me.

So I am satisfied
Just sleeping here with you
While listening to the falling rain
And the beating of your heart.
I have learned to love both

As if somehow
They were one in the same.

Raven Dances
The Grand Canyon National Park 1997

On the edge of the rim,
Overlooking the canyons
Filled with shadows
And waltzing ravens,
I spin the medicine wheel of life
Once more.
Connections awaken within,
Drawing me back
Into the canyon lands
Of unfinished dreams.
Native drummers,
My warrior brothers,
Call out from the shadows
And pull me back into
The canyon lands of desires.

My spirit knows this moment.
It has lived it many times.
I know my way well,
I have been here,
Struggling in the shadows and dreams
Of this canyon land.

I watch the rain
Foolishly jumping
From the sky,
Thinking suicide thoughts
As it falls into the darkness
And melts into the dream-earth.
Only then does it realize
It will eventually have to return
To the comfort of the clouds.

It can never die
In the canyon lands.
It will always be a part of the sky.
I realize that
The dreams will continue
To go on
And on
Until I
And the rain
Desire no more journeys,
No more earthly dreams,
No more deaths
Or suicide jumps
Into the canyon lands below.

Men are Not Mountains

Men
Are not mountains.
They can erode away
From the
Tides of life
And
From silently shed tears,
Which
Pound on the shores
Of their soft hearts.

They are not mountains,
For they cannot stand
So tall
When all alone.

Church Steps

I pause
At the steps
Of an old church.

I guess I am still looking
For that certain moment,
That special feeling,
That magic
Of divine madness.

I am still a seeker,
Regardless of what you believe,
But I want to discover
My own truth.
I want to know
My own God
And not just read about Her
In books written by
Very old dead men.

Conversations with Mirrors

Who are you?
Do I really know the you
Standing so quietly in my mirror?
Thinking that you are not me,
You hang onto the edges of the glass,
Seeking oneness with the light.

All your dreaming and desires
Confuse me
And cast doubts on what I see.

There is no logical direction
To all those moments spent
Navigating the horizons
While pretending to not know each other.

I know the memory of moons and roses,
And wars, and deaths, and battles for the heart.
We were there, even if we did not
Recognize each other.

Ego? Higher self? Shadow?
It makes little difference
When this shell is cast off
In some homeward bound
Stream of light.

I want to embrace both of us,
But I know one of us is only a dream,
Only a reflection on a pane of glass,
Hiding much pain and fear
But filled with so much love.

You and I
Are really but one traveler
Wearing different masks.
The one that everyone thinks they see
Is nothing but a minefield
Of puzzles
And tears.

So we continue
On our journey of discovery,
Full of hope,
Trying to become what
We were created to be!

Journey Back to Light

So many uncharted
And forgotten voyages within,
Hazy memories of dream dwellers,
Silhouetted Navajo men and women
Standing half naked
Around circles of fire.

Stones, feathers, and old dry bones
Hidden in exile
In womb-like hallows
Carved into the bellies of the earth
By the gods themselves.

Ravens and bear
In altered states
Of belief and dreams
Dance with the dreamers.
The fragrance of wet earth
Coming from a curtain
Of thunderstorms
Just outside
The visible shadows of the cave,
Calms the dreamer and beasts alike
As old men talk to the gods
In languages
We can no longer understand.

And ravens
Whisper of journeys
To distant stars
Where the protector of cobwebs
Weaves clouds of white silk
Where wonder begins

And where
There are no hard edges to reality,
Only dreams and visions
And passageways
Leading back to the light
From the darkness.

Costumes

You were hiding
Your real feelings
And thoughts,
Costumed as a smile
And a muted laugh,
So that I only knew
Where the shadows fell
And not the source
Of the light.

I do not know
What you really taste like
When love is hungry
And the moon is full.
Nor what you
Really might feel like
Wrapped between
My protective arms
And the darkness.

Take off your costumes
And expose your soul,
So that I
And the world
May experience
The real you.

Beaches

I stood on the shores
Of Vietnam
And saw blood-red sand
At my feet,
But I never ran away
From the tide.
It was my karma to stay
And wait for the tides
To change.

Life is nothing but beaches.
Sometimes they are rocky and wet.
And sometimes they are too hot
Even for young lovers to enjoy.
But they are all just beaches
Where the tides come and go.
It is all in the attitude.
Nothing more.

UFOs in Central Park?

There are crop circles
In Central Park.
And some Messiah
Carrying a sign
That reads, "Will work for Food & Wisdom,"
Is preaching
In clandestine chat rooms
On the Internet.

I find it hard
To believe anything anymore
Unless I see it first on
"60 minutes"
Or on "Dateline."
I think the whole world
Is falling apart,
And if I am really very lucky,
They will not tax me
After I am dead.

I wish sometimes
That Peru
Was reachable by subway
And that the signs
On the subway walls
Were really written
By the prophets.

I wish Elvis
Was still making records
And that The Beatles
Were still together.
But lately,

I would be happy
Just having enough hair to comb.

It just seems
That if we could put a man
On the moon,
Then why not a woman?
It seems that some things
Never will change.

Was O.J. really framed?
How about Roger Rabbit?
Did Billy Clinton really lie to us?
Can you trust any stranger
Or any naked man
That promises you roses
Without any thorns attached?

Life does not come with
Any instruction book
Or guarantees.
And you know,
I am told
That none of us are getting out
Of here alive!
Except of course,
Elvis
And me
And
JFK.

Vacation Memories

Vacationland dreams,
Still playing out
On the video monitor
Of my heart
With dancing visions
Of desert views
And canyon walls.

They keep me sane
On cold rainy days at work
As I ride their memory
Down rivers of peace
In search
Of angels and ravens.

No Golden Roof
Naples, Italy, 1965

My house has no
Golden roof.
No silver linings
And marble floor.

My house was not
Built for just one,
But at times
It seems
Just the right size
For one lonely heart.

My house sits on
An endless horizon
Just beyond your
Limited view,
Just beyond
The chains
And walls
That imprison
Your soul.

My house is not
For sale.
There can be no price
For the peace
I find within.

My house is built
With threads of lovely
And bricks of joy,

So that on rainy nights
I do not cry.

Thoughts While Hitchhiking
Zurich, Switzerland, 1965

Inside I starve for
The harmony of
My thought-dreams.
I sit alone
Inside myself
Like a butterfly
Waiting to emerge
From its cocoon
Of delusion.

I seek no goals
Of money-world laughs
Or sex-nights without love.

I want no more
Materialist traps
To ensnare me in their web.

Home—is where my soul rests.
There are no manmade walls
Or roof to hide my fears.

Bed—I sleep with myself
Without regret
Without fantasy dreams
Of worldly things.

Alone—yet
Very much together
With sky, wind, sea,
And sleeping visions
Of God's love.

I Sit in the Darkness
Japan 1967

I sit in darkness
Trying to burn holes
In some faraway galaxy of dreams.
My efforts at enlightenment
Appear much like
Rays of sunlight
Captured in a bell jar
Full of love.

The neocortex altar
Of my brain
Cries out
From the edges of the light
And holds off the darkness
One more time.

Rosary Beads
Big Sur, California, 1969

I need no rosary beads
When my neurotransmitters jump
And dance with the sky,
When my spine
Feels like an electric cord
With energy bursting to be free.

The light within
Flies and soars
With the eagles
Over the forest of incense and joy.

I feel no fear
And know no darkness.
My inner candles are burning!

Photograph Image Within
Rome, Italy, May 1965

His face,
Like the sea washing dry shores
On some distant beach,
Wet my memory and spoke to me
As if all my lifetimes
Were only but this moment in passing.

His eyes,
Two piercing magnets
Where worlds swam within,
Stared through me
As if he knew me
In the past, now, and in the future.
Those fiery eyes,
Burned holes in my heart.

I felt no need
To ask the stars
Or consult the cards.
I knew all my questions,
Asked and unasked,
Would be known
When they needed to be.

I realized
That I would never
Have to journey alone again
Because
My Jesus
Walks with me
On lonesome roads
And the crowded detours of life.

Even if it is only
On a photographic image
That I carry within.

Mary
October 1962

Mary,
Fertilized by divine love
In flower gardens
Beyond the dreams of men.
I've felt your wet face
Within me crying,
While on TV
I saw angry crowds
Carrying your Son's flaming cross
Last night
In some little known Mississippi town.

Mary,
I saw your children,
Wet brown eyes and black faces,
Hiding in the shadows
Cast by a burning cross.

Mary,
Forgive them again,
For what they are doing
To all your sons
On this cold Mississippi night.

Monks Do Not Fear Darkness
Cambodia, 1967

The emptiness that can surround you
In the shadows can ingest the whispers
That spring forth from within,
Muting those inner messages
That remain unheard in the darkness.

Meanwhile,
Old monks sitting cross-legged
In cold stone temples
Just stare,
Unconscious of time,
And unconcerned
About sequences of delusion or pain,
Their chi not blocked by fears,
Nor unconscious desires.

They are able to resurrect
Their divine self.
Like lightning chasing the wind,
In altered states,
They just sit there and receive the light
That falls all around them.

Wildflower

We walked together
On that hillside of color,
Stopping only briefly
To take a flower.

The other flowers,
Waving mutely
In the soft wind,
Held back their tears.

Now looking at the vase
Sitting on our table,
My heart is troubled
By our robbery
Of something that cannot
Ever be returned.

Solitary Journeys
Japan, 1967

We each have our own beaches.
But for some
They have never learned
That two sets of footprints
In the sand
Bring more joy
Than solitary journeys across time.

I will awake tomorrow not knowing
When the tides will come or go,
But willing to stand
And let the sea wash over me.

There will always be beaches
And more tides.
So why worry about how much
Sand slips away from the shore.
The tides will return it all back again
Some other day
On some other beach
For someone else
To discover
In some other lifetime.

The Rain Falls

It makes little difference
To the rain,
Seeking an audience
Of fools or saints,
Roses or garbage,
It just falls.
All need the rain.

God's love is like the rain.
It falls everywhere.
The roses don't need to cry out
From their dry beds,
Nor do the children
Who trust in blue skies.
It will come and bless them all.

There are no favorites,
No special deals,
No bribes or payoffs,
It makes no difference who you are
Or where you hide,
The Rainmaker will
Find you just the same!

Angels R Us

The earth and the sky
Could never know
Such bliss within
As I sit here
And observe this moment
Outside of myself
But not alone.

I feel angels within.
I can sense the wind from their wings
And joy from angelic hugs
As blissful waves
Of energy run up and down my spine.

I know no logic
Nor mathematical formulas
For what I feel.

I just wonder sometimes
If maybe
ANGELS R US!

Gypsies and Butterflies

Let the gypsies run naked,
If they wish,
Through the poppy fields
And meadows,
Chasing shadows
Cast by the sun.
They will never catch them,
But they will keep trying anyway.

Let those rebel butterflies
Tease young lovers
By flying over the horizon
In search of rainbows and sugar.
I do not care what is beyond my touch.
After all, I've got you.

I do not need new worlds to conquer.
I haven't fully explored us yet.
I do not need butterflies and gypsies
To teach my heart joy,
I have you
And we have us!

Indian Cliff Dwellings
Arizona, 1997

Sky people,
I see your fingerprints
On the canyon walls.
Your adobe homes
Still cling to Mother Earth.

From your lofty perch
You could touch the sky,
And perhaps,
On a clear desert night,
Touch heaven.

The coyotes and mountain lions
Knew better than to intrude.
Only the raven
Could dare to venture near.

You tried to become one with
Both Mother Earth and Sister Sky.
But you were bound
To the shadows of those cliffs.

What happened eight-hundred years ago?
Where did everyone go?
You left no clues.
Did brother snake tempt you
With some forbidden fruit?

I can only look
And wonder
Where you are tonight.
What would you tell me

If you could?
Would you tell me to leave?

I give you my love,
Ancient brothers of the sky.
I hope you found
Whatever it was
That you were looking for,
When you left your cliff-side Eden.

The Piano Man

I remember that old piano music
Played for lonesome men and drunks
In smoke-filled bars
Where no one ever came to listen,
Drinking their joy instead
From glasses filled with lost hope.

The piano man would try
To fill those empty spaces between the notes
With his own dreams
That were still unspoken and unrealized.

So many moments can drift by
Without ever asking or demanding
Of our dreams,
Like old piano music
Playing endlessly within all of us.

I wonder just how many more songs
Must be played
Before the piano man
Attempts to realize his own dreams!

Winter Chill

The cold winter winds travel
Much too close to my heart.
I want to avoid the inner freeze
That may be coming,
Those dark, icy moments of lonely
That live in the darkest shadows of the mind.

I need sunshine this time of the year.
I need you at this time of my life.
I need to know that warmth can be found
And that there is still
Sunshine behind
All those dark clouds of despair.

I am putting on my winter disguise—a smile,
Just for you, I will try.

I reach out to you in the darkness.

I will be all right, once I thaw out.
I just need your warmth and your love
To help me make it through
One more winter night.

But didn't I always!

Guess I always will!

Quasimodo

I see your inner child
Hiding in the darkness.

Do not try to lie to me.
I am not totally blind
To dreams of hope.

Even clowns cry.

You are not alone.

Get off your rooftop,
And join the world.

Bach didn't sing the blues
Unless the entire symphony played.

You are never alone
Even when dancing
On rooftops.

Look within,
Young Quasimodo,
The sun is shining there.

Do You Really Hear Me?

I can whisper softly
And you just might hear
What I really mean,
If it was what
I really meant to say.

I could speak of times gone
And moments yet to live,

But I chose to clothe the silence
With only emptiness
In hopes
That you will hear
What is not said
By me.

Reunion

I seem addicted
To being in love
With you.

Conquering you
Is all I want to do.

I get impatient with calendars
And clocks when they separate us.

I am disenchanted
With the rest of the world,
All I care about is us.

So I wait,
Hungry for your embrace
And the feel of your warm skin.

My imagination
Feeds on its own dreams
And will have to hold
Me over until
You are emptied
Once again
Into my arms.

Not Enough

My heart has hands
That want to hold you.

My eyes
Have feet that wish
To walk all over you,
Exploring all the unmapped
Regions of your body.

My fingers want
To press against your soft parts
And have them press back.

But all this is not enough,
It will never satisfy me
Because I have only allowed myself
To know your body
And not your soul.

Until I fully explore
Your heart
I will never know
Either one of us.

Security Blanket

I have sewn you
Into the fabric of my heart.

It beats as if we were one.

I look at you,
So quiet on the outside,
And wonder if you are
Dancing joyfully on the inside.

I know I can hardly contain myself
From smiling all the time.

When I unwrap myself
From you in the morning,
It is like abandoning
My security blanket.

It is hard to let go.

Sabotage

Your love sabotages
Any thoughts of anger.

My thirsty heart
Could never remain
In the ripples of uncertainty
Without wanting to experience
You once again.

So I silence
My tongue
And my head
And let my heart soar.

Submarines

Cynicism is like an iceberg
On a collision path
With your heart.

I cannot help but wonder
How deep your feelings go.

Are we still on the surface
Exploring the cold waters,
Or are we ready to be
Like submarines
In search of hidden
Underwater wonders?

The Image in the Mirror

I remember looking in the mirror
And seeing only me.

My image
Was like a button
Holding my soul-clothing
Together.

It only quietly
Stared back.

I waited
For time to change what I saw
And for answers to come.

But it seems
That the image in the mirror
Still looks like me.

And there are still no answers.

Handyman

I wish I had words
To make things right
Between us.

There are things
That need to be mended
And fixed.

But I have never been
A very good handyman,
Always had to hire someone else
To come in to make repairs.

I wish there was someone
In the yellow pages of life
That I could hire now
To repair the damages
That I have done.

So until then
I hope you can live
With my efforts at repairing
All those things between us
That might need fixing.

Besides,
I come very cheap
And have a lifetime warranty!

Minefield of Emotions

I am not so brave,
Regardless of what you've seen.

Medals in Nam
Do not mean a thing
When it comes to facing love.

The fear of losing someone
And being alone,

That is one big minefield
Of emotions
I have never had to walk
Before you came into my life.

Now I am afraid
Of losing you.

The Wind

How can you ignore the wind?
Standing up against its very push
You begin to feel its cold fingers
Stealing your warmth
And your desire to be outside.

Lonely is the wind
For it knows no friends
Except kites
On March afternoons
In the park
And puffy white clouds
That need to move on
To other skies.

Surface Roots

We do not talk
Much anymore.
No more
Dancing,
Holding hands,
Sitting, watching
Our lives unfolding.

No commitments
Beyond the silence.
No red roses,
Candlelight dinners,
Or hungry embraces.

It is all just
Surface roots.
Nothing deep enough
To hold us upright
When the winter's wind rages
And the rain comes.

Risk Taking

Seeking safe harbor,
I sailed
With faith alone
Into your embrace.

What will I find there
Once my heart
Drops anchor between
Your arms?

A quiet lagoon?
Or hurricane-driven seas?

Which Way?

Oh dear friend,
Which way will you go?

So many highways,
Pathways leading to more roads,
Detours heading to dead ends,
Or uncharted worlds.

So many choices,
What will you do?
Where will you go?

Will you ever know
For sure
What was best
And which was destiny?

Does it really matter
Which road you journey?
Don't all roads
Lead to enlightenment
Eventually?

Just choose one.
Any one that you desire,
But be sure
That your inner compass
Is pointing in the right direction.

The Dancers

I could hear the shadows
Slowly moving in the darkness,
The silhouettes of dancers
Moving and whirling
To unheard music.

Divine movement
Outside of mind
And thought,
Just one with the dance
And the body.

I was so alive
Just watching
And experiencing joy
While wondering with envy
About the oneness they felt
With their dance of life.

Children Dance

When I was much younger
I used to dance in my kitchen
And reach out for my mother's arms
To whirl me around
And make me feel loved.

Now I am older,
No longer a dancer,
No longer reaching out
For my mother's arms.

I stand and watch others
Dancing to their own music
While I observe
And grow tired with old thoughts
And dusty dance floors.

It Has Been a Long Time

When did we last snuggle together
Under a blanket
While watching the sunset
Over some lonely beach?

How long has it been since
We were willing to dance naked
And not pull the curtains
Of life
Down all around us
To hide
From the eyes of the world?

How long
Are we both willing
To accept today
Without remembering yesterday's fire?

You were my dream
When dreams were what I lived for.
Now I accept a paycheck
And mortgage as my reality.

How long is a long time?
How many lifetimes
Spent in dreamland
Without ever questioning
Why must we endure?

I miss us
And those daydreams
Filled with poetry
And wine.

How much longer
Must I live in the shadows
Of your heart?

City Streets

This morning,
While driving through the city,
I saw a man
Who used to be somebody's child,
Some mother's son,
Walking in the shadows of the street.

He looked back
At me
Looking at him.

Then turned away,
And with the help of his friends,
Jim Beam and Johnny Walker,
Staggered down the alley
And into the darkness.

My traffic light turned green,
And once again I was headed
Back to my home
In the suburbs.

I checked my rearview mirror
Only to see
Just my own reflection
Staring quietly back
At me.

But my thoughts
Were still walking
With that early-morning man.

Summer Mornings

Why let summer mornings
Stagger away
From blossom-bouquet people
Because of dark secret showers
Of doubts
From within others.

Tell Sister Sky
I am blue and full
Of life.

My love song still plays
But with only
A small evening slice
For you
After all is consumed
By the stresses of my day.

Working in the City

In the middle of the city
Masses of individual people
Become nothing but mindless mobs,
Walking and pushing themselves along
The edges of reality.

Shoulder to shoulder
In silence they march,
Onward toward
Subways and bus stops
That will take each of them to
Their own daily hells.

Some allow themselves
To become voluntarily chained
To some company bonus plan,
While others sell out their souls
For government pensions and a 401(k).

And yet, some just serve out
Their 20-to-life sentences
In their present jobs,
Without the possibility of joy!
And never even question why.

I Read Somewhere Once

Be kind to others.
Do good unto others,
Or something like that.

I never really knew
What book I read that in,
But my heart
Knows that it is truth.

My heart never needed
To read any books
To know
That giving love
Was always better
Than not.

Peeling Onions

Wrapped in soft conversations,
We begin to peel away
The many layers
Of darkness and doubt
That have infected
Our relationship,

Only to discover
It is much like peeling away
Layers from pungent onions,
As tears
Cascade like waterfalls.

Finding no escape
From your staring moist eyes
And my own self-judgment,

I whisper
I love you,
In hopes
That you love me too.

They Say

I am closer
To death today.

I am older
And beginning
To decay.

Any minute
Could be my last.

So I
Submit to
The joy
Of each moment

And abandon time
To those
Who still
Wear watches
And keep planning calendars.

Unrequited Love

Love can hurt
When you are
Left chasing shadows
On the barren ground.

It is hard to see
Rainbows when it
Is still raining.

Love can be difficult
To give up on.

So I continue
Seeking my own
Inner sunshine
Whenever I can
On cold, dark nights

And wait
Patiently
While the sun
Pushes the shadows
Across the hard, dry earth

That I moisten
On occasion
With a few
Soft, wet drops
From my heart.

Found

In my searches
For meaning
I found you.

Or was it you
Who found me?

I was lost
In my own maze of doubts
And delusions

I was forever
Running into walls
And dead ends
Until
I found us.

Before

I only regret
All those days
I wasted
Before
I knew us.

They are now
Only catalogues
Of events and emotions
Waiting to be buried
In some memory cemetery.

There were no colors then,
All was gray
And meaningless.

Even the sun
Wasn't as bright

Before you came.

The Ice Queen

She was like
The fresh virgin snow
Laying there
All naked and cold.

Beautiful on the outside,
But so cold within
That one could get
Frostbitten
By trying to get too close.

But they say
That even
Ice Queens
Have their melting point
During the heat of passion,
So I wrapped her
Very gently between my arms
In hopes that my warmth
Would melt some of that snow
And ice.

Restless

A few more
Roads ahead
I haven't seen.

So I keep
My restless heart
Moving
From lonesome city streets
To empty country roads,

Looking,
Searching
For something
Outside of myself.

Or perhaps
I am
Just running
Away.

My restless heart
Knows no difference.
It just wants
To keep moving.

No time
To stop
And figure things out.

I am scared
Of the thoughts
I may discover within.

And so
I've got
To keep moving

Like the restless
Shadows
Cast by the setting sun.

Airport 2001

Why do airports
Always manage to lose luggage and people,
Leaving lovers and friends
On different coasts?

Airports have become
Nothing but highways of lonesome times
And dying salesmen,
Metal detector minds,
Long lines, rude ticket people,
Hyper children, crying babies,
Oversized seatmates
Squeezed into undersized seats,
Followed by a dinner
Of a coke and a bag of peanuts.

Sitting here at Chicago's O'Hare
(It could be LAX,
Who can tell the differences anymore?),
Waiting and growing much older.
My flight is delayed once again
As I began to feel
Like a hostage in hell.

If angels really do fly,
I am sure they would take the train
Or even the bus,
And avoid airports altogether.

Breakfast Conversations

I look over my newspaper at you
Sitting across the breakfast table
(It could be from across the universe)
And wonder where the passion went.

I pick up the milk carton (low fat milk)
Half expecting to see a photo of us there
Listed as "Missing or Lost."

"So how is your work, dear?"
"How are our children?"
"Is it really going to rain today?"

Just small polite conversations
Over cereal and coffee.
Before we rush off to join the world
Of the commuter-traffic zombies
All going to work and wondering why.

Earth Angel

We lost an earth angel this week.
No more will her smile invade
Our hearts except through memory's door.

Her sunset filled
The darkness of the night,
Leaving us all alone
With only our candles and prayers
And little understanding of why.

I know I will never be able to
Look at a sunset again
With a dry eye
Or without some discomfort
In my soul.

There is a hole in the darkness
Where she escaped
From the depths
Of her despair.

But she will never have to
Be alone in that darkness
As long as those who love her
Continue to remember her.

For love is the eternal light
That never fades!

Auto Mechanic

To her
He was more
Than just some auto mechanic,
But a seasoned explorer
With surgeon-like hands,
Stained as they were
By tattoos and oil.

She would allow him
To grease her joints
And check under the hood.
She trusted him
And didn't care
If he ever wore gray flannel stripes
With wingtip shoes.

She loved his boyish smile
That would break the silent interludes
Between his firm embraces.
She was his woman.
And he was her man.
What more could matter?

Abandoned

The sea is a little deeper tonight,
The waters feel much colder,
The surface more dangerous.

Since you left,
No beach ever feels secure anymore.

Under my feet,
Cold, wet cemetery sands
Sink into footprints
That follow
My solitary journey
In search
Of new horizons.

The Desert

Every desert
Is but an orphaned beach
Abandoned long ago
By ancient seas,
Thirsty sands
That still dream
Of ocean embraces.

I am much like the desert
When we are apart.
My thirsty heart
Still dreams of your embrace
As if I were trying
To reunite my soul
With some missing part
Of myself.

Be Real

If you could see beyond this face
Into these lying eyes,
I could dare to become naked
And free.

If you could know,
For just a brief moment,
The real us,
Then we could learn to soar
Above any earthly scorn.

If you could be me,
And I you,
Just for a glimmer of time,
We might understand
Who we are.

If you could read my poetry
And understand verse and word
What I was attempting to say,
Then there would be no more need
To hide in the shadows of my poems.

If you and I were honest
And sane
Then the moon and sun would truly shine
And time shared
Would mean so much more.

Inner Skies

Under inner skies,
That only can be seen in dreams
And touched in old memories,
I still try to climb
Those same emotional mountains
That we left unconquered.

I am left
Seeking the answers
From the signposts
Of my heart
Because I can no longer trust
Mystical sages
Or angelic messengers
No matter how wise or enlightened.
These answers need to come from us.

After all,
It was we
Who built those mountains.

So, I stumble along many
Uncharted emotional roads
But never alone,
For you are on this journey with me.
Even if it is just under
My inner skies.

School of Light

The temple door
Hides the light within
I can not find my inner mind
While watching the universe
From the outside.

I must venture within
To seek out those prophets
That live in
My cosmic dreams.

Life changes nothing
If I never
Open my heart
And only believe
What I see
As real.

Distance Between the Births

I walk that distance
Between the misty visions
Of birth
And death.
Having
Heard the sounds
Of creation within,
I reach out
In hope
That it will
Lead me
To the light
Of the saints.

Where there are
No more
Wars of the heart
Nor
Anymore tears
To stain the soul
With
Births and deaths.

Journey of Doubts

My thoughts
Struggle with the repressed visions
And memories of things
I do not understand
And create a pathway
To the sacral areas
Of my mind.

I spend moments
Seeking the symbolic connections
Between man
And the stars
And plastic holy figurines
On dashboards
And
Images reconstructed
From a whirlpool
Of childhood dreams.

However,
I sense
There are places beyond today,
Sanctuaries that suggest
Peace could be real,
Where there are no boundaries
For the turbulent heart
That must keep running
Between
Birth and death
Across abandoned fields
Of time.

Desires

Old doubts
And fears
Guard the doors
To enlightenment,
Eluding all attempts
To enter by force.

I know that the light is within.
I can see it
Leaking from behind locked doors
And darkened skies.

But what life force I have
Is still busy
In the womb of desires.

What is beyond
This cave of memory and darkness
Needs guidance,

Some guru of love
To lead me through
A labyrinth of fear
In search of my lost
Yellow brick road.

So I wait patiently
In the darkness
For the light.

Circular Lights

In my mind,
Float memories of
Circular lights moving overhead.

They have seen me naked and alone.
They were there to hold my hand.

Was it love or science?

I continue to wait
For them
To return me
To those chambers
In the white temple
Where no angels dare go
And none call home.

Perhaps,
They will find me
Once again,
Naked and alone,
And take me back to
Where altars of light
Replace time.

I Found Different Shores

I've never
Walked on the shores
Of the Ganges
Nor stood
On the summit
Of some Himalayan peak.

I've never sailed
Down the Nile
Nor climbed
The Great Pyramid,
And Mayan temples and ruins
Are just daydream visits.

But I've sat on the bloody shores
Of the Saigon River
And found great peace within.

I meditated from the cliffs above Big Sur
And watched the ocean
Pounding away far below me.

I have no magical answers
Or even understand all the questions,
But I do know this:
I have been able to find peace
And closeness to God
In all the places
Of my heart.

Perhaps, God
Is not found just in those special places
Where men have journeyed

But where men can dream
And become one
With the peace
That is within
All of us.

Poets Have Faith
and
Believe in Everything

Once when the windows were open to my empty mind,
Truth ventured out from within,
Pouring itself into an empty room
Where no man ever sat nor any thoughts
Were ever written for bold peering eyes.

It is said that poetry begins to kill
That silence in the very moment
It believes it is more than the sleeping reflection of life
That it paints with words.

Old poets know no other way than to memorize
Volumes of prose within, daring not to spend them
In lonesome moments or sense-driven journeys of the heart.

Young poets see only empty rooms and empty minds.
Failing to grasp the blinding light within,
They venture off down roadless highways of thought.

Thinking that thoughts are life,
They leave their words, like dying embers of fire,
Along the side of life's crossroads.

I have learned to see beyond the empty room
Where one can dream of wordless poetry
Written on pageless books, sitting on bookless shelves.

Younger poets than I, go your own way,
Take whatever route gets you to where you are.
I do not want to travel those roads again.
I want nothing more in my empty room.

I am satisfied with what I have not.
I desire no more.
I desire even less
At times!

I am satisfied!

You Were My First Love

I remember you standing beside me
So much younger than today.
Your hair was flowing like water
Over your soft shoulders,
All black, not one gray hair.

I can still see you standing with me
In the morning light.
And your hair still flows like angel tears.

Your eyes still behold me,
And mine you, even after all we have been through.

I guess that is what it is really all about, isn't it?
I cannot think of a better gift to get
Or to give—than being us.
In all these years, that is all I ever wanted or desired.
I have never wanted more than you are.
That is enough joy for me.
I am just glad that you feel the same about me.
And that we both still look forward to tomorrows
And do not seek after our yesterdays.

Well,
I might be slower,
Even balder and heavier,
But I still got you, babe,
And that is more
Than Sonny can tell Cher!
Thanks for memories
That we are going to continue to create.
Thanks for being
A part of *us*.

I Wonder Where Elvis is Tonight?

I listened to some old, dusty records tonight.
Didn't play no tapes or CDs.
Old classic Rock and Roll sounds much better that way.

I could see a vision in my mind's eye
Of Elvis standing nearby.
Not the fat, over the hill, drugged-out, and life-burned-out Elvis.
No, this was the younger one.
The one with sideburns and moving body parts.

He was a god back then.
He would have bought you a pink Caddie, if you had asked him.
He seemed to have it all. The world was at his feet.
We all wanted to walk and dance in his shoes.

I miss you tonight, Elvis.
Once life was so much simpler. You were my idol.
We dreamt together while Ike played golf.
Where did we all go wrong?

Elvis, did you die for our sins on the crossroads of fame?
We took you down that highway of ego
Where love became a drug.

I miss yesterday's dreams. I miss 1958
And your Blue Suede shoes.
I miss Bill Haley and Buddy Holly and American Bandstand.
I miss it all, Elvis!
Are you really dead?

So long rock and roll summers
With ducktails and grease-covered hair.
Death is for mortal men, not an Elvis,

But you were never one of us.
You will never be dead, until I say so.

So it is only good night, Elvis,
And not good bye.
As long as you live,
So do all my childhood dreams.

So it is just good night, Elvis.
See you in a few years.

My Friend Went Back to the Stars

My friend left here.
Went off looking for God's divine fingerprints
On the solar systems of dreams.
Weaving love with moments of color and sound,
He shares space with angels and UFOs.

My friend left this time and place,
Traveling far beyond tomorrow.
Who will remember his earthen-clothed bones
That now lay under the footprints of generations to come?

I will not complain of empty spaces and places
And missing moments as long as I know
And believe that he is not far from my thoughts.
He can never die in my heart,
And is always within visions and dreams
That I can see and visit nightly.

My friend traveled this way,
Passing by on his way to the stars.
I know his journey was not lonely.
My friend stepped out of this time and place
To be somewhere else, perhaps
My limited vision blinds me
And he has not really gone
Anywhere at all!

Was it all a dream, my friend and me?
Was it ever so? Only just an illusion,
A little dream-play of God's?

I thought that dream was real.
Didn't you?

I cried when time vanished behind a veil
Of darkness and death
As my friend found his own pathway
Back to the stars.

I miss
My friend.
It still hurts,
Even if it was
Only but a dream.

The Sea Gives Back

The sea receives
All that the rivers can give,
Then she returns
It all back
Again and again
To dry hills
And to the valleys
Far from shore.

Traveling
As dark rain clouds,
She
Ventures off
To nurse
The earth
With the only love
She knows
She can give.

Does anyone
Ever stop to thank her
Or to ask why?

Words are Only Vehicles Between Moments in the Silence

I can whisper softly and you just might hear
What I really mean, if it was what I really meant to say.
I could speak of times gone and moments yet to live,
But I chose to clothe the silence with only silence
In hopes that you will hear what is not said by me.

I know nothing for sure and sometimes even less.
How can I see your point of view
If you are blocking my vision of my own dreams.

I want to tell you so very much.
I want you to understand and know me
Without me having to speak or write a thousand words.
I want you to feel and see us heart-to-heart.

There is much more to the understanding of me or you
Than words can express.
Words are not a door to the heart.

Trust in the silence.
I have said too much already.
I can hear the silence.
I can feel the invisible chants from silent butterflies
In the soft blue lotus-skies.
I will wait for the silence.
Will you?

The Sky Follows Us
It Never Asks Why

Light seems to fall all around us.
Did you wonder why?
Not even the gypsies
Know for sure.
So, it is no surprise
That lovers seek out
The darkest corners of the room
To hide
Their animal desires.

But the darkness
Is not always ready
To Invite others into
Its closed womb.

Darkness may seem
Like your best friend,
Sleeping so comfortably
With your lustful dreams,
But do not trust
That light-voided world
To give you much
Except shadows
Cast upon darkness.

Darkness is no friend
To those who search
For truth.

Seek and know
The source
Of the light!

The Pathways Are Not Always Marked With Signposts

I met someone once or twice
(Or was it a thousand times?)
Who told me that
He had the only truth,
And the only true path
To find God.

Failure to listen to him meant
Damnation and eternal
Everlasting punishment in the end times!
My soul
Would be lost
In the flames
Of some hell-like place
That he recreated in
Great detail to me!

I was cast with
Hitler
And Judas,
Both of who,
He told me, went to hell,
As well as all those Jews
Who never carried the cross,
Along with those Mormons,
Buddhists, and Hindus.
And of course those Scientologists
Hiding out in LA
With all those yogis
And gurus.
All of who were going to be
On the first busload to hell
When time ran out for all of us.

I assume this makes him feel good,
Knowing that God
Will make others suffer
While he sits at the Lord's side.

I should thank him
For his concern,
But I will travel down my own road
And hope that I do not get mugged
By this self-righteous soul
Who believes that only members
Of the right-approved religion
Are destined to get into heaven.

If that is true, then I thank God
For I am going to enjoy the company
A hell of a lot better
Where I am going!

The Owl Angels

Greeting me from above,
I saw two pairs of eyes
Looking down upon me
From the ledge
Of my office building
In the early morning fog.
It was just two owls
Sitting there.
Waiting, perhaps,
Just for me
To come near them
To share the moment.

Perhaps, they really were just angels
Who had flown in on those tiny wings
And now they were watching over me,
Two witnesses to my life this morning.

Creatures of the night,
Why do you bliss me so
With your poetry of flight
Across the dark sky with your frozen blank stares,
Are you really there?

Do you see something beyond today?
Sequestered there above me,
Patiently like a guru.

How much longer, wise old owls,
Before I find the pathway
That leads me back to the land
Of owls and angels
From where it all began?

When do I get to go home?

Angels, A-bombs, and the Wind

Standing here beside you,
I feel the wind as if angels were cooling the air
With their angelic wings.
All the heat that passes in anger
Finds relief in the morning breezes.
All the tears that have fallen in lost moments of doubt
Shine like sunlight off angels' hair in the wind,
And I feel peace once again,
Even when faced with world news headlines,
"The French Drop Another A-bomb!"

God is everywhere today,
Even in that hole the French ripped through the blue sky and sea
With their atomic-sized egos.

I know not anger but concern.
I know not fear but wear the face of pain.
I do not believe in yesterday, but I have some hesitation
About what tomorrow may bring.

So I stand alone, naked of anger and judgment,
In the angelic winds,
Trusting that love is the only power that lives forever.

Come join me in solitude and hide your mind
In the shadows of my heart.

I will hold you close to me
While angels cry in radioactive clouds
Above some blue hole
Where sea and sky
Once lived together.

The Past is Dead

Remember is a long-time word,
Deeper than Death Valley sunsets.

I need not fight with memory,
No more.
It is a choice
That I have made
To let the dead leaves
Fall to the ground
And get blown away
Like a season in my life.

I know that
Even as the rains come and cold winds blow,
The newness
Lies just under the ground,

That seeds left months ago now only sleep,
That green
Leaves will replace
Those that have fallen
And have blown away
From my past-life world,

That every season
Brings changes,
And that all
Must experience
The past in order to have a future
That is bridged with many todays
And many fallen leaves.

Emotions are Just Tracks of Tears

I sleep with my eyes open sometimes,
Yet no one knows.
I cry within sometimes
And hurt when no one else is looking.
I yell out from my silence
Every now and then.

I sometimes even
Run naked in my shower.
You weren't watching me
Were you?

I have had times
Both good and ugly and that is not so bad.
I can still feel the tender of the night,
And I know all the words
To "Blue Moon."
By the way, what in the heck
Does doo-wop mean?
I guess I have seen most everything
In my day except
Finding that light at "the end of the tunnel"
I've been looking for since Vietnam.
Perhaps the light
Is within me?

A Dream Without Any Sunshine

I found
Churches without any doors.
As I wandered
Between eternity
And the shadows,
Trying to remember
That photograph image
Of a universe within.

It was from
That edge
Of the horizon
Where I was neither
Dead nor awake
That I cried out
From the crawlspaces of memory,
Asking
God for His sunshine
To remove the shadows
Of Eden
From my heart.

Clouds Do Not Own the Sky

Nature has many ways
To show its love.
You and I
Know but just a few.

We will never feel
What the rose feels
When the softest sunrise
Dries the dew
From the reddest of rose petals
And green tender leaves.
Nor will we ever know
What love the flower feels
To be the residing queen of the garden.

Oh, sometimes
Clouds may try to steal
Moments away from the sun,
Pushing blue sky out of view,
But we know
That it is only a matter of time
When butterflies and sunshine
Will grace our view once again.

You and I
Can only patiently watch
And hold hands
While we wait.

Points in Time

There seem to be points in time
When memories serve no good purpose
Except to feed fears and doubts.

When what you dream
Is so much better than whatever was,

The real can become unreal
And life seems but just a dream.

I stand alone, naked at times,
And sometimes emotionally wearing
Even less for protection.

There are times when
I wish to avoid the cold hard truths.

Some things are best not remembered at all.

Time Will Tell

I do not understand why the sun
Warms up the fields each springtime
Nor why flowers grow from seeds.

I do not understand how my computer works
Or all that it can do.
I know even less about my wife.
What makes her tick?
What does she think about?

As I grow older
I understand and know so much less.
I can still not comprehend
Why there are wars
And why there is so much hate.

What makes a young boy
Join with other children
And give birth to a gang?
Why does the IRS
Always want more of my money?
Why do football players
Make more money
Than teachers and nurses and moms?

Why are there homeless and shoeless children
Walking the streets of LA and Chicago?
Where did we go wrong?
Did we all go to sleep
And this is all just a bad dream?

I do not understand very much anymore,
But I do know about love.

That is the only thing
That life has taught me.
Love is all I really ever understood!
Perhaps,
There is nothing more
We need to understand.

He Might Have Been a Saint

I never thought that much about him
Until he up and died one day
While everyone was sleeping.

He never said much when he was alive.
It was often hard to tell if he was
Really dead or alive,
Most of the time anyway.
He hardly noticed much that happened
Around him each day.
I used to wonder why he never
Watched the six o'clock news
Or read the USA Today.

Something is very strange about any man
Who never watched a football game.
He did not know a Ram from a Raider.
And didn't know there were Saints
In New Orleans.

Heck, he never learned
About the president being a pervert
Or that the Spice Girls broke up.
This guy just didn't have a clue
About all that sin in Washington, D.C.
Nor the violence in the streets.

What a poor soul he must have been
To never have worried
About wars, crimes, or his next meal.
He just took life as quietly
As he could.
He missed out

On all that good stuff
That the rest of us know about.

I guess he did not understand
What life was all about.
Just lived his own,
So quietly and sheltered
You would of thought that he was a saint
Or at least dead
At a
Much younger age!

Tibetan Words Chanted Within, in an Overture to God

I can feel you as one with the rain.

All of life is in rhythm with the rain

People come and go.
Some dance on the shores
And grind wet sand between their toes
In hopes of touching that vast sea.

The sea receives
All that the rivers can give
And returns it back again and again
To the shores
In rain-filled clouds.

No one ever stops to ask why.
No one seems to notice the never-ending cycle
Of life-giving rain,
Of births
And rebirths.

The sun comes up
And it leaves us again.
Each and every day
It gives us life and growth
Much like the sea.
It too is a never-ending cycle,
And no one asks why.

That is the natural rhythm
Of the sea and the sky.
That is the cycle of life,
And not many ask why.

There is no death
In the natural wonder of things.
There is no finish,
No last sunset
To all that ever was.
Only many beginnings
And many rainy
And sunny days!

Awakening!

I am ignorant of doctrines.
I sleep only with my own thoughts
To guide my soul in its journey home.
What feels right needs no endorsement
From the Pope or a saint.

The mystical Kingdom of God is within all of us.
It cannot be found without effort,
But love does open the gate to forgotten pathways.

I feel much today,
But I know
That any dialogue with the wind
Will not create any inner peace.

I seek wisdom from Socrates and Mohammed,
Christ and Buddha,
And even Bob Dylan.

But in the end, I know,
There are no Egyptian sunsets
Or mystical magic
That can enlighten either one of us.
It must be all discovered
Within our own selves.

Inca Medicine Wheel

I was walking in my dreams
With Inca anthropologists and Amazon prophets
Among self-realized shaman
Who all stood silent and naked
In a hidden jungle temple.

I was seeking something more tangible
Than just Eucharist sacraments
To feed my hungry heart.

The moonlight,
Like some schizophrenic transfusion
Of awareness,
Danced around my dreaming head
And focused my thoughts
On my own apocalyptic visions
Of thunderstorms and fear.

I looked around
And saw only old yogis
Bleeding their spiritual DNA
Into red pools
That gathered at the feet
Of crucified apostles,
While soundless music filled the air.

In the distance
Slept over one thousand ancient theologians.
Not realizing how close they were
To the medicine wheel,
They continued to shout out
From their many scriptures and sutras
And never looked up

To see the Inca sunsets
And the divine moments of magic within.

I awoke
And cried out for all of us
Who have lost that inner vision,
Who do not believe in dreams
Of old Inca shaman
And jungles
And medicine wheels.

No One Can Really Know Paris
Paris, June 1965

No one
Can really
Ever know
Any city,
Ocean,
Forest,
Or place
Unless
They become one
With those
Who live there
And love there
And die there.

I know,
I tried.

Saw a Young Child

I saw a young child today
Playing by himself.
But he was not alone
In his moments
Spent
At the park.

He shared
His joy with
All who saw him.

He needed no one
To tell him
When to smile
Or laugh.

He knew
The world within
And the world
Around him
As only a child can,
By imagination
And a willing openness
To believe
And accept.

Fabric of Life

Lots of people wander around
Visiting many parts of the world
But fail to experience anything
Beyond memories of places
And their own personal thoughts.

The fragrance of joy
Needs to become a part
Of our fabric of life
As we dance across incarnations
In search of ourselves.

We can never experience
More then we are able
To give of ourselves.

We seem to spend all our time
Seeking to absorb memories
Of places on postcards
And in movies,
Failing to stop
And question why.

We need to listen
To the soft whispers
In the winds,
The chanting of birds,
And the gentle cry
Of the sea
As she rolls
Across the beaches
Of time.

I can never
Be satisfied
Only seeing places
And hearing songs
Played by others.
I want to become
A part of the moment
And sing the songs too!

Inner Poetry is Not for the Critics

I would love to just be myself
Once before I die,
Allowing myself the total freedom
To create prose
From thoughts hidden
That reflect who I really am.

But it has never been
The right time
Nor the right place
For such personal poetry.

I wanted to be somebody
When I was a child.
Now, all I want is to be me.

When is there going to be
A coming-out party
To honor all those poets
Living in fear of disapproval.

I have poetry within me
That must wait until the darkness
To climb out of my heart
And bare its very soul.

I am not ready to charge across
This world
With my underwear always exposed
And my thoughts
Always subject to cross-examination
By those who think
They know me.

Critics do kill
Any desire to run naked
With the truth.
So, there is nothing to be gained
By letting others crawl around inside me.
They will never understand
My poems.
But, I have hidden these inner poems far too long.
These rebel thoughts now howl
At the very fabric of life.

I am who I am.
No more than that.
I will always be me.
Even if no one else
Knows who that may be.

I wish to remain
A mystery
Hidden within myself.

Perhaps,
The words of my poetry
Might give me away,
But I will never tell.

I am who I am,
But I am not
Who you think
I am
Or should be.

About the Author

W. H. McDonald Jr. is a poet, author, and founding director of **The American Authors Association.** He was part of the flight crew for the Vietnam War documentary **In the Shadow of the Blade.** His autobiography, **A Spiritual Warrior's Journey,** was first published in 2003. His book of war-related poetry, **Purple Hearts,** was published in 2004. His poems have appeared over the years in print publications and online.

Bill is a Vietnam veteran who did his tour of duty with the 128th Assault Helicopter Company in South Vietnam, from October 1966 through October 1967. He was awarded several medals including the Distinguished Flying Cross, the Bronze Star, the Purple Heart, and 14 Air Medals.

He earned his B.A. degree at the University of San Francisco and his A.A. degree at San Jose City College.

He is married and lives in northern California near his grandchildren. He also does abstract oil paintings. He supports various foundations and causes and makes himself available to speak to organizations, clubs, and associations. He is also a part-time wedding minister.

If you wish to contact Bill, you can write him at this address:

Bill McDonald
Post Office Box 2441
Elk Grove, CA 95759-2441

His web site addresses are:
The Vietnam Experience   **LZ Angel**
www.vietnamexp.com   www.lzangel.com

His e-mail address is available at either website.

Made in the USA
Monee, IL
12 March 2023

29501572R00085